# LETTING GO

## THE HEALING POWER OF FORGIVENESS

STUART SEBOMBO

Letting Go,
The Healing Power of Forgiveness


ISBN: 978-9913-610-06-3



Cover design and layout by:
Angels Camp

# Dedication

To my mother, Rebecca Nabikolo Sebikejje.

Thank you for living out forgiveness. Thank you for teaching me to love and forgive. I am who I am today because of you. I love you, mama.

# Contents

Dedication ........................................................................3

Introduction........................................................................5

PART ONE

Chapter One: What is Forgiveness?.................................................14

Chapter Two: How do you know when you have forgiven?.............35

Chapter Three: Forgiveness, a gradual journey or an instantaneous leap? ........................................................................40

PART TWO

Chapter Four: Forgiven by God .......................................................49

Chapter Five: Benefits of knowing how much God and others have forgiven you........................................................................58

PART THREE

Chapter Six: Why should I forgive others? .......................................68

Chapter Seven: 12 Benefits of Forgiving Others...............................82

Chapter Eight: Forgive Yourself .......................................................85

# Introduction

At about 5 am one morning, I awoke to find six missed calls from my mother; this was not like her. "Did we lose someone? Perhaps she sent a message," I thought to myself as I frantically scrolled through my phone to confirm my suspicion. What I found was even more ambiguous! "Something has happened; please come home as soon as you can." Wow, Mother! I immediately called her back and, when she picked listened to an audio relay of her text; something has happened; please come home as soon as you can. At least there had been no sobbing in her voice. Having reasoned that the option of death was improbable, I got ready and got home within the next 2 hours. Once we had reached the formal salutations out of the way, I was given a front-row seat to the latest unremarkable tale of family drama; my cousins had fought, and the older, bruised and hanging onto a sack of gold had imprisoned the younger. The cause of the fight was a pile of rubbish - literally! Despite my biased position toward the two, I took on the role of protagonist! My part was simple; since I had nothing to do with the fight (or so I thought), I would go to the police station and calmly negotiate the release of the lad. I would then mediate their reconciliation amidst much laughter and tears of joy. I wasn't ready!

The anger and hatred in that tiny police office next to the prison were so tangible we needed the police detective present at all times lest it turned into a murder case! The bare-knuckled fight had unearthed several years of pain and mistrust within the family. My grandfather made an appearance, too, albeit by correspondence from the heavens. Baseless accusations way beyond the pointless brawl ensued amidst shouting (and inevitably spitting) sweating and threats going back and forth. By this time, the protagonist, too, was well in on the action! If it had not been for the detective's timely interventions, there would have been blood on the floor, and nothing resolved. How had we gotten this far as a family?! We were so blind to the frustrations and blame we held towards each other that it took a rubbish fight to let it all out. I am grateful that it was also through this event that we went on a journey of forgiveness and true reconciliation.

We all need forgiveness at one point in our lives. As long as you breathe and interact with people, you will get the fantastic opportunity to be offended by or to offend someone, whether consciously or subconsciously. Worry not if this hasn't yet happened to you. It is only a matter of time. However, we should never forget that holding onto the hurt caused by our teachers or parents, spouses, bosses, friends, yes even ourselves, has only one beneficiary. His name is Satan. We partner with the real thief, the devil, to fulfill his purposes whenever we choose not to walk in forgiveness.

The thief comes only to steal and kill and destroy; I have come that they may have life and have it to the full - John 10:10

Satan is **never** for you. He will do everything possible to steal from you, kill and destroy you, and one of the ways he subtly does so is by convincing you to hold onto offense. He is the chief of sowing discord (lack of harmony) among brethren (Proverbs 6:19).

When you choose to forgive, you prevent those seeds from bearing fruit. When you decide to forgive, you unite friends, and you redeem relationships generations beyond that would have been sabotaged before ever starting. You partner with God in destroying the works of the enemy.

He who covers a transgression seeks love,
But he who repeats a matter separates friends
- Proverbs 17:9

I, Sebombo Stuart, son of Rebecca, would be dead or rotting in prison somewhere if it were not for forgiveness! I would have been expelled from school for cheating or plagiarism, beaten to a pulp for stealing, or even lost my business for messing up assignments and relationships.

I have experienced forgiveness!

I know what it means to hear someone you've wronged say, 'I forgive you and grant you another chance to try again.

There are moments the weight of my own mistakes has overburdened me, seasons where my guilt suffocated me to a point where I felt too powerless to get up from bed and try again! I know I would never have made it to where I am if not for people forgiving my faults. I would never have had the courage and confidence to speak up or lift my head and dream again, dream even more significant if the chains of guilt and condemnation had never been cut off my back, by those that forgave me when I erred, the very ones whom I hurt by my actions!

I have seen what forgiveness does to a soul. My sincere desire for each human being daily carrying the burden of past hurts, or being overwhelmed by the guilt of past mistakes is to give or receive forgiveness, let go and experience the healing power of forgiveness.

You, too, can experience that same freedom and victory if you understand forgiveness's healing power.

I hope that as you read this book, your heart shall let go of that weight of unforgiveness that you carry, no matter how justified you think you are, to punish those who have wronged you by waiting for them to pay up. May you champion reconciliation in your family, be an ambassador for the restoration of dignity to those trapped by their guilt and replace the shame that comes from self-condemnation with the glory bestowed to a slave set free. May you remember that forgiveness is available to EVERYONE and fulfill the mandate given to you as a child of God to reconcile the whole world to Himself. Reconciliation and restoration start with forgiveness.

And while at it, may you be guided by the words of Ivern Ball*;*

Most of us can forgive and forget; we just don't want the other person to forget that we forgave,

and learn to LET GO. It is a function of you, not the offender.

In a world full of imperfect human beings, I have learned to take charge of your joy and peace, choose to forgive, and be humble enough to seek forgiveness if only to maintain the relationship. The closer a person is, the greater your expectation for perfection, the more excellent the opportunity to be offended, and hence the more vital your resolve should be to forgive.

I have learned that sometimes we are stuck in life simply because we or someone failed to forgive. Hatred and anger punish great-grandchildren for the sins of their fathers, the bastard son carries the guilt of his parents' errors, and the teenage mother has the burden of shame and at times even animosity toward her beautiful blue-eyed daughter; FORGIVENESS!

When you forgive (or receive forgiveness), you open the doorway for healing and restoration to flood in.

If the healing for our broken world were in one of the rooms of a house, and we were stuck outside in a hailstorm, the one key that would give us access through the main door is forgiveness!

# Part One:

# Demystifying Forgiveness

Everyone says forgiveness is a lovely idea,
until they have something to forgive

Mere Christianity (1952) by C. S. Lewis

# Chapter One: What is Forgiveness?

## According to the Dictionary

The root of "forgive" is the Latin word "*perdonare*," meaning "to give completely, without reservation." The dictionary defines to *forgive* as;

- grant pardon for or remission of (an offense, debt, etc.)
- to give up all claims on remit (a debt, obligation, etc.)
- to grant pardon to (a person), to cease to feel resentment against:
- to cancel an indebtedness or liability of:

Interestingly, all these definitions focus on the offended party instead of the common belief that the offender takes precedence in seeking forgiveness. To forgive is to give up the desire or power to punish. Forgiveness involves granting, giving, remitting (debt), or pardoning (an offense). It is natural for you to want the one who has offended you first to feel the same pain you felt or understand what you have gone through before you forgive them. We often want the person to take the first step and seek us out, weeping and begging for forgiveness. While this may show the state of the offender's heart, forgiveness is ultimately a function of the one who is offended.

## According to the Bible

To understand what forgiveness is, we have to understand; ***Punishment*** *- the infliction or imposition of a penalty as retribution for an offense.* Understanding punishment is crucial because *we only forgive those found to be guilty or who admit faults.*

If we confess our sins, He is faithful and just to forgive us our sins and to cleanse us from all unrighteousness - 1 John 1:9

The scriptures give us a picture of God's idea of forgiveness;

For God so loved the world that He gave His only begotten Son, that whoever believes in Him should not perish but have everlasting life - John 3:16

Forgiveness - a choice to give: In John 3:16, we see that it was destined for destruction when the world disobeyed God. God, out of the abundance of His love, CHOSE to give His only begotten Son so that the world would not perish. He did not have to, but He decided to anyway when He offered up His Son as payment for the debt we owed due to our sin and did not wait for us to seek Him out. God showed us that the offended one ought to offer forgiveness whether or not the offender has asked for it. The offended one holds the power to offer forgiveness. The world did not petition God to send Jesus to die on the cross. There was no representative from the world in the committee that chose the way of the cross, showing us mercy and paying the price for our offense. It was not in the amount of weeping or length of days of fasting that He chose to pay our debt! No! It was solely from His heart. The one who was offended decided to offer forgiveness. What is left is for the offender, the world, to receive; *whoever believes in Him*!

But God, who is rich in mercy, because of His great love with which He loved us, even when we were dead in trespasses, made us alive together with Christ (by grace, you have been saved) - Ephesians 2:4-5

Forgiveness – is about the person, not the offense: The origin of God's forgiveness is His love and compassion toward us, and so should ours be. The offender (person) is more important than the offense. God loves people, desiring that none perish. God so loved that He gave; because of His love for us, he forgave! In remitting our debt through the perfect sacrifice of Jesus Christ, He overpaid so that the issue would not be how great our sin is but rather how great His love for us is. That is Forgiveness!

There is a reason why it is easier to forgive/pardon those we love when they wrong us than strangers. It is easier to condemn another woman's son whom you see on the news than your own, even when before God both might have done something that carries the same punishment. We even make up reasons to undermine the offenses of those we love just, so it is easier for us to forgive them and retain the relationship.

"It is about the person, not the offense!"

Over 2000 years later, God's forgiveness is still available to everyone who believes in the Christ He sent, to the thief and murderer alike! It is a blessing to receive forgiveness.

> Blessed is he whose transgression is forgiven, whose sin is covered – Psalm 32:1

We should take this same posture to forgive truthfully; Do we genuinely love the offender? Are we willing to be the ones to offer a way back into a relationship even when the offender is blind to their offense? Do we understand the eternal consequence of our refusal to forgive the transgression?

Forgiveness – is free: because this world's economy runs on the concept of buy and sell, it is difficult for a man to accept that the gift of forgiveness is entirely free. Many people, even believers, struggle with the idea that God has freely forgiven all their sins, and there is nothing left to pay to earn His forgiveness but to receive! The Bible says that;

> And be kind to one another, tenderhearted, forgiving one another, even as God in Christ forgave you - Ephesians 4:32

In the same way, God has forgiven us, FREELY, we ought to forgive others.

Forgiveness is limitless (it can be for anything): the covenant between a husband and his bride, or the relationship between a father and son; are for a lifetime (no contracts). The parties involved have to decide beforehand to extend limitless forgiveness; how much they are willing to pardon (the weight of offense), and how many times. You cannot guarantee today was the last time your son messed up and hurt you. But you can create an environment where they know that however great their mess might be, they are always welcome to learn and rebuild. And no, there is no guarantee that they will not abuse that opportunity, but the Lord himself did the same for us!

## The Luminous Baited Hooks

It was almost dark, and Sebastian was still missing! Two hours since handing over the money for the new carbon-steel black nickel-coated luminous hooks, and nothing heard from him since. Peter had greatly anticipated this night. The possibility of making up for all the previously missed six fishing nights due to Sebastian's obfuscation was quickly dwindling! If only he could sell some fish in the morning, he'd have some money to leave home while on the trip! "Why do I keep trusting this lad?" Peter muttered under his breath, increasingly growing impatient! A few moments later, under the biting cold, Peter called off the fishing company, sending everyone home. Once again, Sebastian had successfully delivered a boatload of disappointment!

I catch up with this story in Matthew 18 *(New Sebombo Version – NSV)* when Peter had given Sebastian a decent beating under holy anger the following day. Now seeking to justify his actions approaches Jesus and requests his thought on the matter.

> Later, Peter approached Jesus and said, "How many times do I have to forgive my fellow believer who keeps offending me? Seven times?" Jesus answered, "Not seven times, Peter, but seventy times seven times! - Matthew 18:21-22

Jesus' answer is precise. Forgiveness is limitless. While Peter thought that forgiving the same person seven times was a stretch, Jesus multiplied that by seventy, indicating the infinite nature of God's forgiveness which we have to imitate.

## The Beloved Bastard Son

Growing up, a few neighbors claimed I was naughty, and it didn't help that I hung around a very *creative* bunch. My mother was widowed only a month after my stately arrival and forced to move back into my grandmother's house, had the uphill task of driving out all the foolishness that was bound up in my little five-year-old adventurous heart. Together with my gang of little rascals, we spent most of the holidays planning mischief.

We explored the outcomes of putting hot pepper in water guns and shooting straight for our playmates' eyes. We composed and passionately presented abusive songs for the mean neighbor who had consistently refused to nourish us with the '*mandazi*' that had overstayed at his shop and provided safe custody to other kids' toys without their consent! All this mischief while living under another's roof!!

The extent of our jurisdiction was too small, though. We often got caught and had a few ceremonial beatings performed in the presence of the offended neighbors. A few days of remorse would follow, and then we'd slip right back into our following scheme.

While I wasn't sure if the neighbors would let bygones be bygones, I had deep-seated confidence that I would still be fed and cared for by my mother irrespective of the side of the ceremony she'd taken prior. She loved me. I would not have to repurchase my way into being her son! I was covered, forever! She did not resent me or use the moments to blackmail me into buying back my son-ship. My identity was secure. Even amidst the tears and determination to get back at the neighbors, I knew that I'd still call her my mother! I knew my mother loved me. I knew I was covered.

Those earlier experiences in my life laid an excellent foundation for what it means when God forgives! To be covered limitlessly. It helped me understand that when I rest in His love, there is nothing that I didn't have to doubt God's forgiveness.

In Acts 7:59-60, Steven forgave his murderers while he was dying;

And they stoned Stephen as he was calling on God and saying, "Lord Jesus, receive my spirit." Then he knelt and cried out with a loud voice, "Lord, do not charge them with this sin." And when he had said this, he fell asleep.

Forgiveness is a precursor to reconciliation: there is no healing without forgiveness, only pretentious relationships marred by gossip and back-biting. Where there is no forgiveness, there is always the suspicion that the debt will someday be collected and, therefore, mistrust and disunity. Forgiveness is the foundation of reconciliation. Without it, there is always enmity for which it only takes a few sparks to explode!

Come now, and let us reason together," Says the Lord, "Though your sins are like scarlet, they shall be as white as snow; though they are red like crimson, they shall be as wool - Isaiah 1:8

But now in Christ Jesus, you who once were far off have been brought near by the blood of Christ. For He is our peace, who has made both one, and has broken down the middle wall of separation, having abolished in His flesh the enmity, that is, the law of commandments contained in ordinances, to create in Himself one new man from the two, thus making peace, and that He might reconcile them both to God in one body through the cross, thereby putting to death the enmity – Ephesians 2:13-16

Forgiveness is love: I cannot claim to love someone from whom I am willing to withhold forgiveness. Jesus directly links our forgiveness with our love.

Therefore, the Kingdom of Heaven is like a certain king who wanted to settle accounts with his servants. And when he had begun to settle accounts, one was brought to him who owed him ten thousand talents. But as he was not able to pay, his master commanded that he be sold, with his wife and children and all that he had, and that payment is made. The servant, therefore, fell before him, saying, 'Master, have patience with me, and I will pay you all.' Then the master of that servant was moved with compassion, released him, and forgave him the debt - Matthew 18:23-27

We, too, have accounts to settle. The Bible says that the wage of sin is death. That is why the only way we access God's forgiveness is by believing in Jesus Christ, in whom God settles all our accounts toward God.

God, moved with compassion in Christ, has forgiven all our debt.

There was a certain creditor who had two debtors. One owed five hundred denarii, and the other fifty. And when they had nothing with which to repay, he freely forgave them both. Tell Me, therefore, which of them will love him more?" Simon answered and said, "I suppose the one whom he forgave more." And He said to him, "You have rightly judged - Luke 7:41-43

## Forgiveness, Repentance, and Responsibility

*Forgiveness* is to the offended (the one who grants forgiveness) and *repentance* is to the offender (the one who receives forgiveness). *Responsibility* means admitting you are not right, admitting your fault.

**Reconciliation** takes both forgiveness and responsibility. Forgiveness alone is not reconciliation; while it is necessary, it is only the fertile soil in which the seeds of repentance bear the fruit of reconciliation.

FORGIVENESS
Obligation of the Offended

RECONCILIATION

REPENTANCE
Responsibility of the Offender

**Forgiveness** is not calling a wrong a right or minimizing the hurt. It is not tolerating the wrong or being indifferent to the evil or the wrongdoer. Instead, forgiveness requires that we;

1. Acknowledge that a wrong has occurred; while we may excuse people because we do not blame them for something gone wrong, we can only forgive people when we admit they earned the blame.
2. Recognize that the wrong created an obligation for repayment; there is always a price to pay when it comes to forgiveness
3. Voluntarily choose to release the offender from that obligation and cover the loss yourself
4. Understand that it doesn't eliminate the consequence of the wrongdoing for yourself; you might forgive the drunk driver that cut through an intersection killing your five-year-old daughter, but unfortunately, that would not bring her back to life. Forgiveness, however, would help you carry that pain without destroying your heart and give room for healing over time.

In Worthington's *REACH* model of forgiveness, we can see all these aspects of forgiveness;

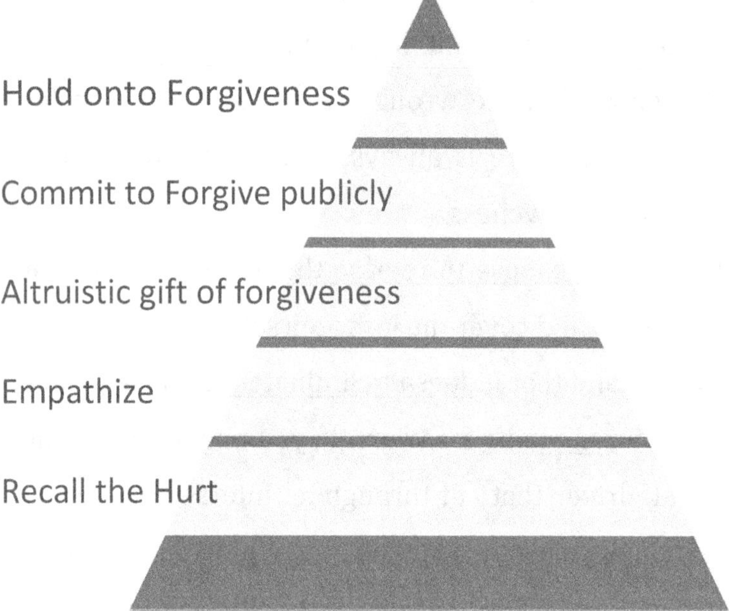


**R**ecall the Hurt: we cannot forgive that which we ignore. We have to be honest enough to face and evaluate the pain, however deep it might be. Do not downplay hurt due to fear of how deeply it might cut.

*We can try to forget it, stuff it into our subconscious where it will become a mole and do its mischief beneath the surface. Or we can forgive it and heal it* – Worthington.

**E**mpathize with the offender: dare to see the person the way God sees them. It is true that, left to ourselves, we cannot love our enemies. It takes the power of the Holy Spirit to see people the way God sees them. To empathize with the offender is to put yourself in their shoes and know the offense with a broader and deeper perspective. It is approaching the wrongdoing with the understanding that apart from Christ, we too are capable of the worst possible evil and then desiring to see the possibility of their redemption as human beings.

*For I know that in me (that is, in my flesh) nothing good dwells; for to will is present with me, but how to perform what is good I do not find*

– Romans 7:18

Mack is sincerely struggling with the idea that God loves His children. Having lost his youngest child Missy, he comes face to face with a lady called "*Wisdom*" at the judgment seat, ready to be judged! Approaching the conversation, clad in arrogance and extreme resentment toward a God who claims to love His people and yet let them suffer, Mack is shocked to be assigned judge. Wisdom invites him to take her place and judge all the different people he blames for all the pain and suffering in the world. That is the opening of the Judgement Scene in the 2017 movie, *The Shack*.

As pictures of the selfish and greedy, those who harm others, murderers, drug dealers, and terrorists, are played back onto a rocky façade before him, he doesn't flinch while quickly condemning the guilty to hell. As the scene's tension builds up, he finds himself trapped after sentencing a wife-beater who turns out to have experienced pain at the hands of their own brutally violent father! He is in a dilemma; He, the righteous judge, condemning an innocent boy battered by a merciless drunken father to hell. The dialogue that ensues through short, effortlessly cut through my self-asserted righteousness, removing any ounce of right or justification not to forgive in my heart!

*Wisdom: What about this boy? Would you judge him?*

*Mack: He is a kid!*

*Wisdom: But you already have! That boy is your father.*

At this point, Mack cannot believe he had just passed judgment on a boy (Mack's father) without giving any thought to the possibility of the seed that bore his father's violent actions later in life.

The judgment scene played back in my head once again in the middle of a heated argument with one of my cousins, let us call it word-war three, to be fair. This time I was the one in the judgment seat! Amidst the heated accusations and threats, I suddenly saw not my cousin, the man in front of me, but rather my cousin, the little shirtless innocent neglected boy still angry at my grandfather for ignoring him on several occasions. Instead of anger, I felt compassion for that little boy. I determined in my heart to pursue reconciliation, even if it meant that I'd have to surrender my carefully aligned arsenal of argumentative venom and humbly ask for forgiveness (even if only for the sake of only reconciliation). It was then that I saw the real enemy. My cousin was only a decoy! The more the real enemy was revealed, so was his secret weapon; UNFORGIVENESS!

We should not have tunnel vision when dealing with forgiveness. The room should be left to consider the person's past experiences and hurts. When we approach the offense with the broader understanding that God did not create anyone inherently evil, it makes it easier for us to see them the same way God does.

It is easy to withhold forgiveness when we do not consider what it is like to walk in another's shoes.

**A**ltruistic gift of forgiveness: remember your own experiences of forgiveness. Firstly, as a Christian, God has given you the gift of forgiveness. Outside Christ, we hell-bound! No excuses for it. Whenever we are grateful for the forgiveness we have received from God and others without minimizing the gravity of our wrongs, it creates freedom in our hearts to extend that same forgiveness. We inevitably walk in humility. A guilty man who has freely received the forgiveness that he did not deserve will most likely, in return, forgive those who have wronged him.

Altruism is love that is focused on others, i.e., giving without expecting anything in return. One of the greatest gifts we receive is the gift of being forgiven—it is freeing and uplifting.

<u>Commit to forgive publicly:</u> tell the person you have pardoned them. As your behavior becomes habitual, it will reinforce the decision to forgive what you have made and your emotions of compassion and love.

<u>Hold onto forgiveness:</u> you have to be intentional about holding onto your decision to forgive. Yes, the emotional stress might resurface upon seeing the offender or when the person refuses to repent. Still, in reflecting on why you forgave and meditating on God's purpose for forgiveness, you can find the motivation to guard your heart against relapsing. The temptation to act on the negative emotions that resurface doesn't mean you haven't forgiven. How you respond to those emotions is what matters. As you focus on the reason you acquit and continue publicly committing to your decision (perhaps with a few people you

trust or by role-playing scenarios in which you'd find it challenging to forgive), you gain more strength and resolve.

Though we have despised God's Word, His servants, and His mission, He has shown us kindness. Empathizing with our humanity (remembering that we are only dust and incapable of righteousness left to ourselves), God chose to pay our debt with the blood of His perfect innocent son so that instead of death, the world would receive life. God keeps the door open for whoever is willing to receive forgiveness and be reconciled to a covenant relationship with Him! And more than 2000 years later, God is waiting for you and me to accept that forgiveness. It is not that He doesn't feel the pain; the only reason is that His love outweighs the pain we have caused Him.

# Chapter Two: How do you know when you have forgiven?

*Lau*del House

Ever since finding out that he had been part of the gang spreading the rumors, I had packed up all the trust I had in people, trashed it, burned the trashcan, and buried it! The betrayal hit so badly.

I remember the night I caught wind of the rumor. The most dreaded label had finally caught up with me, and indeed it stung and stunk! I rolled up in my decker bed and continued painfully digesting a recap of my past few weeks as arduously delivered by one of the private investigators a few decker beds down the line. I was so sure I heard clearly; Stuart is '*Lau*'! Could it be that I had finally made the headlines? For a moment, I thought perhaps they meant the other Stuart. The anticipation for clarity made it worse since we were only two Stuarts in the whole school. Such a small sample space to escape that bullet! However, these being my dorm mates, albeit not well-trained in the art of whispering, I was a bit confident that they were gossiping about another person, and that gave me the courage to wait it out until morning.

The rim (gong) went off, and up I was, the events of a few hours ago shortly interrupted by my lack of enthusiasm to approach the basin. Those would be the last sights of the free world for the next few years or so!

*'Lau'* meant gay (not happy) in school, and I was in a boys-only boarding school. To be accused of being *lau* was a death sentence. A *'lau'* senior one student, simply diabolical! My petite frame and the soprano voice worsened things; I collateral damage before the war. I didn't know what to do about the accusations. The false allegation sank me!

That was one of the worst moments of my life. It was not because of the accusations; I had seen boys survive those and regain their star status amongst the other boys. It was the betrayal of some of my friends who kept silent, left me out to hang, and avoided me like the plague during that season! I coiled up!

Today I hold no hard feelings toward anyone from that era but honestly, it took me a long time to let it go.

I would secretly wish they'd fail. I hoped that each one of my accusers, taunted by their guilt, would one day come pleading for forgiveness for stabbing me in the back and leaving me dead all those years ago. I was like that drug addict who'd celebrate a week or two of being sober only to be found in a dark alley the next day, relapsed! Even while at university, armed with those scars of battle, I'd wish some of them would finally realize their error and reach out fervently apologizing remorsefully over the useless words they spoke.

I do not know when the forgiveness came full circle, but I noticed changes in how I responded to the friends who had hurt me;

1. ***Reference not pain:*** I no longer talked about the experience with pain in mind but instead used it to draw more lessons
2. ***No desire to retaliate:*** I stopped desiring revenge

3. ***No Hiding, Confront Conflict:*** I found no need to avoid people anymore. There were no violent encounters played back in my head because there was no more desire for revenge
4. ***God loves them still:*** The Bible says that vengeance is the LORD's. As much as I know this to be true, the inclination of my heart was the desire for the ones who offended me to understand how much God loves them. I knew that my being offended had not reduced God's love for them one bit.
5. ***Generosity:*** I found it easy to give to them without thinking about the pain they had caused before

## Story of Joseph and his brothers

In Genesis chapters 37-50, we find the story of Joseph the Dreamer, the beloved son of Jacob. As a young man, Joseph's brothers get jealous of Joseph's dreams and decide to get rid of him by killing him. By the grace of God, they instead sell him to a group of traders who, in turn, sell him (must have beehigh-returnturn commodity) to Potiphar, a leader in Egypt. He is unfortunate to be wrongfully accused by his boss' wife, which leads him to prison before being released to lead the nation of Egypt, only second to Pharaoh!

Joseph was sold into slavery when he was about seventeen (Genesis 37:2), and he was thirty years of age when he became vice-regent to the Pharaoh (Genesis 41:46). Not many of the readers have lost **thirteen years** to their siblings' betrayal. Joseph could have chosen to either;

- numb the pain (meaning depending on his mood on any given day he'd retaliate against his brothers) or;
- plot an executive serving revenge for every year lost (he was not short of resources)

However, in chapter 50, we see him weeping over his brothers and being generous toward them instead with no intention of taking advantage of their misfortune and rubbing it in their faces how they hurt him.

He even acknowledges the hand of God, taking away the responsibility for the pain he experienced from his brothers and instead choosing to see the love of God even in their wrongdoing.

Like Joseph, we, too, can truly experience offering forgiveness to those who have hurt us and be set entirely free.

# Chapter Three: Forgiveness, a gradual journey or an instantaneous leap?

Forgiveness is both an ***occasion*** and a ***process***; forgiving the offender is an occasion while finding relief from your pain. God doesn't ask us to come back in a week or two and check on the progress of our forgiveness requisition. His forgiveness is instant, and so must ours be.

Forgiveness is both psychological and emotional. While the shock and anger may linger, we have to decide beforehand that our default setting is forgiveness, no matter the offense. If you wait for the weight of the rage to determine how long you hold onto the grudge, you will not be able to forgive immediately. Just as salvation is instantaneous, and then we daily take the journey of transformation, pressing on toward the mark of the high calling, so is forgiveness. God does not wait for us to be utterly perfect before He forgives us. He knows that only in Him are we found to be perfect.

The same is true with forgiveness; the more we delay offering forgiveness, the longer the period for the anger and pain to subside. While the negative emotion attached to the offense might come forth whenever you replay the situation mentally, they should find your resolve to hold onto your position to forgive if you experience the joy of completely letting go.

## 'My Mzee'

Growing up, I pointed fingers at almost everyone around me but myself for every curveball that the world threw at me. I had a point-and-blame kind of list that allowed me to take no responsibility for writing my life story then. Unfortunately, my loving grandfather featured on that list quite often as a child. Now, before we move further along, allow me to create a bit of perspective.

I had the kindest grandfather one could ever want. I searched for him in numerous ways. He was a very brilliant man and yet so humble. He always knew how to re-establish peace whenever someone in the family stirred up mischief. His voice was so gentle and yet so firm with immovable authority. No matter how naughty I was as a child, he did not dwell too long on the subject. Not that he shunned discipline, he but was quick to restore my status as his lovable grandson and always made me feel welcome in his home even when I was not on my best behavior. Sometimes I would wonder when he would sneak up on me and finally explode, but he never did! However, amidst that admiration, there was a brief season in my childhood when I felt strong resentment toward him. Suffice it to say; he had no idea that I felt that way throughout that whole period!

A perverse man sows strife and a whisperer separates the best of friends - Proverbs 16:28

That was the case concerning the source of my deeply baseless resentment toward my grandfather. Whenever my mother was short of money for food or every time I saw her struggling to keep us afloat, a perverse man would rise up and wittily point my little fingers in the direction of the source of our struggle.

"Your grandfather should have given his daughter a better education. She would not be struggling this much," he would say.

"Why the mansion (except it was not even close to one) when he sees that you are struggling in one room?! He does not care at all!"

Such were the words that echoed in my heart after that every time I saw my grandfather drive by. At times I would wonder how selfish a grandfather could be. Had he missed the grandfathering auditions? Did he not get the memo? Every depiction of a grandfather on television was the opposite of my experiences and dug deeper into my pettiness. A real grandfather would have sold his clothes just to have me enjoy my best ice cream, I'd imagine sometimes! It was his duty! Every time the echoes rang out in my heart, I ached with anger at how duped I had been to think that he cared one bit for me.

I was so fully convinced in my heart that if my grandfather had cared enough while raising my mother, then we would have had a much better lifestyle. I gathered up the little strength I had left in me and took my rightful place on the bench. The warden blindfolded my grandfather as he led the latter to the defendants' table so that he wouldn't harm me upon realizing that I was responsible for sentencing him to the next few years absent of his grandson's (yours truly) unmatched love for him. I felt his pain, too, knowing how broken he would be. Nevertheless, I had to do it. If not for myself, at least for my contemporaries who were silently suffering the same fate. I was ready to die a martyr, the voice of reason for the oppressed little boys whose grandfathers did not care enough to carry them high on their shoulders every once in a while! At least I still had the perverse man to thank for illuminating my mind with who my grandfather was.

What a fool I was in doing so! And no, the drama did not unfold that way.

What broke this resentment was the respect and honor I saw my mother show her father. I asked myself why I was so angry for something that did not even happen to me, let alone not being sure whether or not it happened at all. Why did Mother love him so much? She was justified in resenting him. My anger was primarily emotional support. Why did my grandfather disappoint my hatred whenever we spent time together? Was he pretending? And the ponderings went on and on.

It's so unfortunate that I resented my grandfather for about nine years. I missed out on nine incredible years of spending more time with a man I, later on, came to admire, simply because I allowed a false witness' seed of strife to take root in my heart, notwithstanding the baselessness of it all.

I am in no position to forgive my grandfather because of all the accusations that the perverse man labored to elaborate on to me. God was kind enough to reveal the former's heart in the latter years before he passed on, and I am so grateful that I got to honor him the way I was supposed to. Not many people get that chance. There is so much good my grandfather did in comparison to my petty burdensome mischief.

I forgave my grandfather for everything and anything he didn't make right and for decisions that he made that caused me pain while growing up. But he overlooked so much more! I forgave myself, too, for wasting valuable time holding onto a grudge I didn't understand in the least. I dismissed the whisperers because I realized that they, too, were nursing pain. Someone had to break the link: hurt people hurt people!

That chapter of my life opened my eyes to see how not forgiving and harboring bitterness not only blurs one's clarity towards a person's true character, especially when one doesn't fully understand their story but also WASTES PRECIOUS TIME.

The sooner it is that we forgive, the sooner we get back the power over our lives! If we knew how short our time on earth is, we would not belabor the issue of forgiveness.

So teach to <u>number our days</u> that we may gain a heart of wisdom

- Psalms 90:12

When we choose to carry the grudge in our hearts and hold onto the pain, instead of giving it up, we lose precious time and act in foolishness. We are prisoners of our own making when we choose not to forgive.

# Part Two:

## The Value of Knowing God Has Forgiven You

When Love Calls You Home by *Commissioned*

Waiting on the edge with your prodigal heart
Wanting for someone to save you from yourself
Out there on the ledge dangling somewhere in the dark
Doubting if anybody really cares
And Your love reached through the shadows
Whispering your name
Nothing will ever be the same again

**Cause when love calls you home**
**Forgiveness embraces the past you once owned**
**And all the mistakes that carried your name are gone**
**Cause that's what happens when love calls you home**

Cradled in the mercy that has no limits
Finally found the place where I belong
Now I can't imagine one moment without You in it
It's hard to believe I tried to make it on my own
You picked me up from the ruins of my broken life
When every chance was spent, You gave me one more try

# Chapter Four: Forgiven by God

## Do I need God's Forgiveness? I do not even believe in GOD!

Firstly, one cannot receive forgiveness from a God they don't believe exists. Nevertheless, before you skip over this chapter, my dear atheist/agnostic/free-thinker brother/sister, if indeed in believing there is one true deity thou may disdain, consider my *simple* personal tale of childish affair and after that perhaps from subjective fatuity you shall refrain;

*Pwaaahh!! First, dead silence then came ringing in my right ear! Mr. Lwanga, the Principal, had perfectly executed the slap!! I, too, was secretly impressed by the well-calculated swing. I had ducked too late. I knew I should have been revising for my English exam due the next day instead of drawing cartoons on the blackboard in front of the rest of the class. I quickly staggered to my seat at the back of the classroom, trying so hard not to cry (which effort was betrayed by classmates' apologies and giggles).*

*Then it happened; just as the Principal was retreating from the class, I got a vision; the ceiling opened up above me, and I could see Mr. Etyang, my science teacher, all dressed in white surrounded by glorious light. He seemed to be saying something but for the ringing in my ears. As the ringing subsided, I heard what he had been mumbling all along. He had been saying over and over;*

*FOR EVERY ACTION, THERE IS AN EQUAL AND OPPOSITE REACTION!*

It is okay to laugh at this point. No one will judge you (you don't believe in God anyway, at least not yet).

Thank you, Mr. Etyang! I'd like you to know that Newton's third law of motion made it into my prayer life if you are reading this.

I could try to convince you about the existence of God through science and creation, or the healing miracles I have witnessed, many of which have been medically impossible to explain, dead people, coming back to life. Perhaps you'd muse at words of prophecy that God has so accurately performed. And yet I pray that in the dead of night, you wake to the sight of a flesh-eating night dancer by your bedside, fork knife, and napkin in hand, eyes fixed on you. Or that you walk into that little bedroom with my innocent cousin's only a few minutes ago calmly reading her novel, now throwing off men twice her size and speaking in my great-grandmother's voice. Or better yet, I pray that you offend that witch doctor down the street, and he puts your ears on your cheeks!!!!

**Why is it so easy to attribute power to the devil and yet doubt GOD?!** If, indeed, Newton and Einstein are your martyrs (read, you believe in the authenticity of science), the existence of good is most certainly proven by the presence of evil. **I hope you encounter the devil, if only so that you believe in the one true God.** Once you meet darkness, you're only way out will be into the light. That is my hope.

Now that we agree that there is only one true God, you and I need His forgiveness!

"If You, Lord, should mark iniquities, O Lord, who could stand? But there is forgiveness with You, That You may be feared."

- Psalms 130:3-4

The Bible says that all have sinned and fallen short of the glory of God! None of us is worthy, my friend. There is no relationship with God outside His forgiveness; the first condition not to be indebted to God, that is, to be in right standing with Him, is receiving His forgiveness! Outside the forgiveness that He has freely given through Christ, none of us qualifies!

What makes God's Love for you and me so great is the magnitude of our sin. How you know your mother truly loves you is not when she forgives you after stealing sugar. No! You might even feel a little entitled to her forgiveness. But show up from university at her doorstep carrying twins instead of that second-class upper, and you'll honestly know how deep her love goes (of course, I am not saying that you go try that out!) The point I am making is God was not obliged to forgive us. He owed us nothing. It was His boundless love that moved Him to send His son to redeem us. We brought nothing to the table!

While we were still sinners, God loved us! While we were still lost in drunkenness and orgies, robbery and murder, oppressing and stealing from the poor, He sent His Son! It is the very sin the devil uses to disqualify you that moved God's heart because of His love for you, to redeem you. He knew that we had no power over sin outside of our relationship with Himself.

You are freely forgiven by God in Christ if you only believe and receive the Christ God sent to die for you and me and reconcile us back to God the Father.

Do not be deceived that you are too far gone! If God could forgive David who murdered his friend and married his wife, Paul, who persecuted the arrested and murdered some of the early Christians, and Stuart who was sexually perverted, what makes you think that He cannot forgive you?! The devil's most lethal weapon is lies; God cannot forgive you or love you. Or too filthy to be saved. Of course, that is a lie from the pits of hell!!

GOD LOVED THE WORLD SO MUCH THAT HE FORGAVE!

And His forgiveness has not run out just because you are now in line!!! God withheld nothing when redeeming us. He overpaid so that we would never be able to undo His forgiveness as long as we are in Christ. Once and for all, He redeemed us. That is the certainty of His forgiveness! When It comes to mercy, He is RICH!

*"But God, **who is rich in mercy**, because of His great love with which He loved us, even when we were dead in trespasses, made us alive together with Christ (by grace you have been saved), and raised us together, and made us sit together in the heavenly places in Christ Jesus, that in the ages to come He might show the exceeding riches of His grace in His kindness toward us in Christ Jesus. For by grace, you have been saved through faith, and that not of yourselves; it is the gift of God, not of works, lest anyone should boast. For we are His workmanship, created in Christ Jesus for good works, which God prepared beforehand that we should walk in them."* - Ephesians 2:4-10

I remember looking down from the gallery, and instead of feeling depressed. I had tried so hard to stop and yet seemed to get nowhere! I felt like giving up. The noise from the young men and women in the nave below sacred me! How had they done it?! Was it even possible for a young man to be pure? So much freedom, and liberty! I wanted to be set free so badly and yet at the same time felt so disappointed in myself that I'd failed the one who gave His life for me yet again! With every bold proclamation that he made, the passionately enthusiastic young preacher continued to peel away at my secrets, violently tugging at my heart from the sanctity of his pulpit. The topic of the day; PURITY!!

Had God seen through the worship leader finally?! Had He eventually bailed on me and revealed my sin to his prophet? Would this be the day that He finally called out, *Stuart, son of Rebecca, come forth! You have been measured, weighed, and found wanting. Begone from my presence, you the double-faced pretentious adulterous excuse of a worship leader!* It was one of the most stressful and, at the same time, most liberating Kairos moments I have ever experienced! Right there, amidst the affirmative cheers of the youthful congregation, perhaps trying to shout over the noise of their guilt, from the layers of multiple shadows tucking away the aisles of the gallery, I made up my mind to stop running away from the possibility of exposure and confront my sin. How?

*You have forgiven the iniquity of Your people;*
*You have covered all their sin* - Psalm 85:2

Firstly, being fully convinced that GOD LOVED ME. Secondly, understand that while some might not have seen the filth inside, GOD KNEW ME COMPLETELY more than 2000 years ago and still took a chance with me. I knew that above all others, God wanted me completely transformed and healed, and from then on started using the story of my journey to purity to lift others and encourage them that it was possible.

The lack of understanding of the love of God for me caused me to live under condemnation even when my heart desired to be holy. I had forgotten that while I was still a sinner, God loved me and gave His Perfect Son to die a shameful death on the cross so that I would be set free. God reminded me that I had done nothing to earn His forgiveness and that nothing I would do could add to or decrease it. Whenever I'd justify my relationship with God through my good acts, the weight of my shortcomings would hit me like a ton of feathers.

I know God forgave me; I don't feel it, I KNOW IT. And for those of you who might still be trying to measure and belittle your sin to fit within the forgiveness you received, get over it. You are more sinful than you'll ever admit and yet more loved by God than you'll ever know.

*Now to the one who works, wages are not credited as a gift but as an obligation. However, to the one who does not work but trusts God who justifies the ungodly, their faith is credited as righteousness* - Romans 4:4-5

# Chapter Five: Benefits of knowing how much God and others have forgiven you

It was a cold Saturday morning when she met me along that dusty village road. My parents had tightly wrapped me in white linen, carefully tucked away beneath three garbage bags with just enough room for me to breathe. Rebecca would have quickly passed by me if not for an ongoing scuffle amongst a conference of flies next door that interrupted my peaceful sleep and caused me to let out a soft cry. "How can anyone dump such a beautiful baby?" she asked herself, leaning over and pulling back the garbage bags to reveal what would be one of the best gifts she would ever receive in her whole life.

I am the '*muggala nda'* of my mother, which refers to the child who 'closes' the womb. My arrival into this world and my father's death are a month apart, confirming my prestigious position as the last born. I have two amazing mothers and five wonderful elder sisters. The garbage dump story, however, was my first recollection of my origin from my dear mother. Whenever I tried to make fun of my sisters while little or exceeded my daily bundle of notoriety, she would sit me down and remind me of how she took me in out of her generous heart, and so I should be grateful. And then she would let through a hearty laugh. Why wouldn't I believe her? It was my mother. She knew me before I knew I existed! Every time she told that story, I would feel so humbled and privileged at how lucky I was that this lovely lady took me into her home and would be on my best behavior until the next neighborhood adventure surfaced. Her method always worked!

Nevertheless, my growth in both wisdom and stature, in addition to my big head (both physically disproportionate to my petite frame then and behaviorally), undermined the authenticity of the garbage story, and eventually, the truth leaked! I was indeed my mother's son by blood, and she could not throw me away! This truth set me free! Unfortunately, it set my creative mischief free as well.

There was a gentleman in the neighborhood I grew up in one of the city suburbs. His name was "mulokole." He was a lean dark man who never seemed to smile and had a mysterious demeanor about himself. Mulokole was a mysterious man. He would leave his house next to the banana plantation every morning and ride to the towns beyond; a wooden box tightly strapped to the back of that wiggly bicycle, followed by the delicious aroma of the mandazi tucked beneath the once translucent polythene. On several occasions, he returned with a few mandazis left and, ignoring our hunger pangs and pleas for his compassion, threw them into the garden. Why taunt tired and hungry four-year-olds with this wastefulness, we reasoned! One day we decided to compose a chorus with a simple message to appeal to Mulokole's kindness. It was a short danceable chorus questioning his cold disdain for the hungry. We simply stated the facts, and the repercussions of not answering our cry, and concluded with crude abuses in the outro. Your boy was the gang leader, and my big head quickly identified when the parents paraded us for identification later that evening!

Imagine the horror on my mother's face getting back home that evening to the news of her beloved humble son not saving her a front-row seat to his maiden performance?!

She would not have it raising a musician (*read disrespectful abusive gang leader*) in her house! I had crossed the line. The neighborhood chapter convened, witnesses lined up and heard, collection pails for the foolishness assembled, and the purging line set up. That evening all my stupidity was uprooted, and the chorus was quickly abandoned.

Nevertheless, throughout the drama, never did I even for a moment forget that I was still my mother's son and that of all the people surrounding me, my mother loved me most.

## Ten benefits of knowing how much God and others have forgiven you

1. Restoration of relationship with God: Your identity is secure. Knowing that God has forgiven you firstly establishes you as a son. Kind David in the Bible is my best representation of one who enjoyed this blessed relationship even through his failures.

David says the same thing when he speaks of the blessedness of the one to whom God credits righteousness apart from works:

Blessed are those whose transgressions are forgiven, whose sins are covered. Blessed is the one whose sin the Lord will never count against them - Romans 4:6-8 NKJV

2. You are grateful. The more outstanding the debt, the more grateful the debtor is when forgiven. It is essential to know how much God (and others) has forgiven you so that you don't get to take forgiveness for granted.

3. You love more: Jesus told His disciples that one who is forgiven little loves little, but one who is forgiven much loves much. *Therefore, I say to you, her sins, which are many, are forgiven, for she loved much. But to whom little is forgiven, the same loves little." (Luke 7:47)*

4. You forgive others: it's easier to forgive others when you know that you, too, have been pardoned. You are free to forgive others when you understand that you, too, have been freely forgiven by God, a debt that you can never repay. *And be kind to one another, tenderhearted, forgiving one another, even as God in Christ forgave you (Ephesians 4:32).*

5. No more shame: you need to know you are now free from the indwelling sin. You are free from guilt and regret.

*There is, therefore, now no condemnation to those who are in Christ Jesus, who do not walk according to the flesh, but according to the Spirit (Romans 8:1).*

6. You enjoy peace of mind: For He is our peace, who has made both one, and has broken down the middle wall of separation (Ephesians 2:14). Holding onto offense causes separation by which there can be no peace

7. You can be vulnerable to others about your weaknesses or failings (and therefore impact them with lessons about or from your faults or failings). This openness then breeds vulnerable-trust-founded authentic relationships. *And above all things have fervent love for one another, for "love will cover a multitude of sins." (1 Peter 4:8)*

8. You enjoy more fruitful relationships with others (if you're feeling guilty all the time, it's hard to enjoy productive relationships with others; you're always self-centered, not others-centered.

9. You gain an eternal perspective: when you understand that you're flawed and needed forgiveness from God, which He has given you, you approach life with eternity in mind.

10. You gain the strength to ask or seek forgiveness from others. Knowing that you have been forgiven by God almighty gives you the power to seek forgiveness from those you have wronged. If the Almighty God has forgiven you much, you have hope that people too can forgive you.

# Part Three:

## The Value of Forgiving Others

**Somebody's Baby** by *Switchfoot*

She yells, "If you're homeless sure as hell you'd be drunk
Or high or trying to get there or begging for junk
When the people don't want you
They just throw you money for beer."

Her name was November
She went by Autumn or Fall
It was seven long years since the Autumn when
All of her nightmares grew fingers and
All of her dreams grew a tear

She's somebody's baby
Somebody's baby girl
She's somebody's baby
Somebody's baby girl
And she's somebody's baby still

She screams, "Well, if you've never gone it alone
Well, then go ahead; you better throw the first stone
You got one lonely stoner
Waiting to bring to her knees."

She dreams about heaven, remembering hell
As the nightmare she visits and knows all too well
Every now and again, when she's sober, she brushes her teeth

Today was her birthday, strangely enough
When the cops found her body at the foot of a bluff
The anonymous caller this morning tipped off the police
They got her ID from her dental remains
The same fillings intact, the same nicotine stains
The birth and the death were both over
With no one to grieve

# Chapter Six: Why should I forgive others?

My father usually says that many of us do not sin because we cannot afford it. We quickly point our mouths toward those who lack wisdom and have the resources to spend on their folly. The Bible says that a fool might appear wise simply because they keep quiet.

Often, we are quick to set the standard of forgiveness because we haven't had the opportunity to examine the cause of a deed. We despise the prostitute, condemn the rapist, and stone the murderer forgetting that their actions are most likely only responses to past experiences and the fruit of the knowledge they have allowed into their minds. That is why we have to renew our minds continually; it is not an involuntary act to set our minds.

Before we consider withholding forgiveness from others, we should examine the genesis of the person's behavior. Assume there was a time the person was not inherently evil or broken; the monster was once somebody's baby girl, and if only we would see clearly, she still is.

## God has forgiven me

The primary reason for forgiving others is because **God has forgiven us.** God's free forgiveness is the most liberating truth if you struggle with forgiving and holding onto grudges. It is enough to disqualify us from withholding forgiveness from anybody.

Because God has freely forgiven us, we therefore freely forgive. With the understanding of what God did for us through Christ's death and resurrection, His expectation is for us to forgive too; ALWAYS!

*If someone says, "I love God," and hates his brother, he is a liar; for he who does not love his brother whom he has seen, how can he love God whom he has not seen? And this commandment we have from Him: that he who loves God MUST love his brother also*

- 1 John 4:20-21

## Am I in the place of God?

*Thus you shall say to Joseph: "I beg you, please forgive the trespass of your brothers and their sin; for they did evil to you." Now, please, forgive the trespass of the servants of the God of your father." And Joseph wept when they spoke to him. Then his brothers also went and fell before his face, and they said, "Behold, we are your servants." Joseph said to them, "Do not be afraid, for am I in place of God?* Genesis 50:17-19

When Jacob died, Joseph's brothers knew that now Joseph would finally surely pay them back for the wrongs they had done to him as a little boy. Firstly, plotting to kill him and then selling him off into slavery, they came up with a strategy to avert any potential revenge. They knew that Joseph had enough resources to pay back with interest. If he had decided that his brothers would sing karaoke by the riverside the rest of their lives, they would have immediately headed for band practice! Joseph had all the authority needed to exert as much pain as deemed fit. But he knew better! He knew he wasn't God.

We, too, should never forget that we are not God! Wisdom is acknowledging that only God can withhold forgiveness if he ever desires.

## The Parable of the Unforgiving Servant (Matthew 18)

*Therefore, the Kingdom of Heaven is like a certain king who wanted to settle accounts with his servants. And when he had begun to settle accounts, one was brought to him who owed him ten thousand talents. But as he was not able to pay, his master commanded that he be sold, with his wife and children and all that he had, and that payment be made.*

The wage of our sins is death. We cannot pay back what we owe God by our actions.

Therefore, the servant fell before him, saying, 'Master, have patience with me, and I will pay you all.' Then the master of that servant was moved with compassion, released him, and forgave him the debt.

Although the servant showed the willingness to pay the debt, the master understood that the servant couldn't settle his account. While our tears and remorse might be the appropriate emotional response to show that we are genuinely sorry, it takes the compassion of God to receive forgiveness. Tears are not the currency that repays debt!

"But that servant went out and found one of his fellow servants who owed him a hundred denarii, and he laid hands on him and took him by the throat, saying, 'Pay me what you owe!' So his fellow servant fell at his feet and begged him, saying, 'Have patience with me, and I will pay you all."

When you compare the debt, it is ten times less than what the former owed his master. Similarly, whenever we withhold forgiveness from our fellow men, we forget that we owed God so much more, and yet He FREELY forgave us!

"And he would not but went and threw him into prison till he should pay the debt. So when his fellow servants saw what had been done, they were very grieved and came and told their master all that had been done. Then his master, after he had called him, said to him, 'You wicked servant! I forgave you all that debt because you begged me. Should you not also have had compassion on your fellow servant, just as I pitied you?' And his master was angry and delivered him to the torturers until he should pay all that was due to him."

Whenever we do not forgive, the Bible says that we are WICKED!

*"So My Heavenly Father also will do to you if each of you, from his heart, does not forgive his brother his trespasses."*

In this parable, we find the character of the Kingdom of God when it comes to forgiveness, the Kingdom of which we are citizens. Your debt has been fully pardoned child of God by the very one you have offended through sin. Therefore, you too ought to do the same for others; forgive, and pardon their debt.

*Therefore*, as **the elect of God**, holy and beloved, **put on tender mercies**, kindness, humility, meekness, **longsuffering, bearing with one another, and forgiving one another**, if anyone has a complaint against another; **even as Christ forgave you, so you also must do**.

*But above all, these things put on love, which is the bond of perfection. <u>And let the peace of God rule in your hearts</u>, to which also you were called in one body; and be thankful. Let the word of Christ dwell in you richly in all wisdom, teaching and admonishing one another in psalms and hymns and spiritual songs, singing with grace in your hearts to the Lord. And whatever you do in word or deed, do all in the* *name of the Lord Jesus, giving thanks to God the Father through Him* - Colossians 3:12-17

For if you forgive men their trespasses, your heavenly Father will also forgive you. But if you do not forgive men their trespasses, neither will your Father forgive your trespasses - Matthew 6:14-15

We cannot claim to be of God and yet be content not to be like Him. Truth is consistent! The same God we know to be merciful says in James 2:13 - *For judgment is without mercy to the one who has shown no mercy. Mercy triumphs over judgment.* We cannot believe that it applies to us and yet doesn't apply to others! That makes us liars!

## The 3R's why I Should Forgive

In Worship Harvest, one of the most efficient tools that we have copied from Mike Breen's material is the UP-IN-OUT triangle. As a student, It has helped me understand what would otherwise have been difficult teachings from the Bible. I shall therefore make use of the triangle to discuss the UP-IN-OUT of why we should forgive others, i.e.,

UP – *Reconciliation,* IN – *Restoration,* and OUT – *Restructuring.*

Reconciliation: God's mission *(Colossians 1:20)*

*"and by Him* **to reconcile all things to Himself**, *by Him, whether things on earth or things in heaven, having made peace through the blood of His cross."*

The forgiveness we receive from God is ultimately for RECONCILIATION; the world into a covenant relationship with God. When we understand God's mission, we develop a greater conviction toward forgiving others. We picture ourselves walking hand in hand on the streets of gold with those whom we could have chosen not to release.

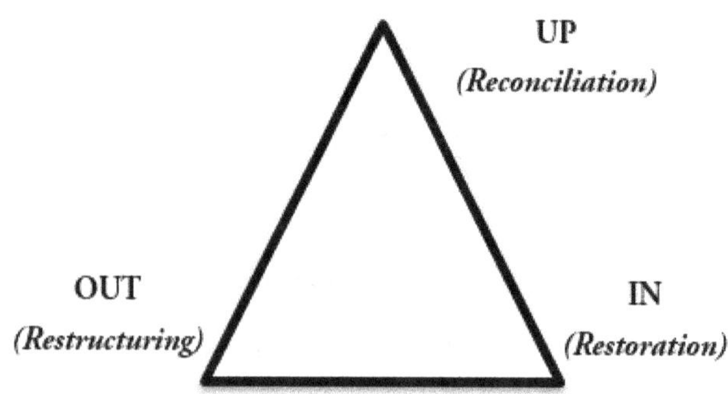

*"If the forgiveness that we received at the cost of the blood of the Son of God, Jesus Christ, is so ineffective in our hearts that we are bent on holding unforgiving grudges and bitterness against someone, we are not a good tree. We are not saved. We don't cherish this forgiveness. We don't trust in this forgiveness. We don't embrace and treasure this forgiveness. We are hypocrites. We are just mouthing. We haven't ever felt the piercing, joyful wonder that God paid for with the life of His Son. I mean, how in the world could I hold a grudge against somebody when I have not been offended like God has been offended — so highly that he has to pay the life of his Son for me to be forgiven?"* – **John Piper**

Restoration: Discipleship *(Colossians 3:13)*

***"Therefore, as the elect of God, holy and beloved, put on tender mercies, kindness, humility, meekness, longsuffering; bearing with one another, and forgiving one another, if anyone has a complaint against another; even as Christ forgave you, so you also must do."***

God sets the lonely in family (Psalms 68:6). These are discipleship families not made up of heavenly beings but somewhat imperfect, flawed human beings, with whom He has entrusted the privilege of growing in the character and competence of Jesus (restoring us to our true identity). Where offense takes root, discipleship cannot happen! One of the best ways to guard ourselves against bitterness is to forgive even before the error occurs. That way, we guarantee that the work of God is not frustrated. An environment that practices forgiveness repels offense and encourages unity among brethren.

Take heed to yourselves. If your brother sins against you, rebuke him, and if he repents, forgive him. And if he sins against you seven times in a day, and seven times in a day returns to you, saying, 'I repent,' you shall forgive him - Luke 17:3-4

Then Peter came to Him and said, "Lord, how often shall my brother sin against me, and I forgive him? Up to seven times?" Jesus said to him, "I do not say to you, up to seven times, but up to **seventy times seven**.

God expects us to forgive every time we are hurt, without exception. When Peter asked Jesus the limit to forgiving a brother, Jesus didn't first seek clarity on the magnitude of the offense committed. Perhaps Jesus would have first asked what the brother had done and apportioned timelines based on how bad the situation was. He instead multiplied Peter's suggestion of seven times by seventy! That is 490 times! How do you forgive one person 490 times for offending you?! By the twentieth time, you'd most likely have deleted their number from your phone and started warning the other brethren about how toxic this brother is.

How do you forgive the $1^{st}$, $2^{nd}$, $3^{rd}$ ......$135^{th}$ time?!!!!! Our LORD desires to leave room for our brothers to repent.

Restructuring: Community transformation *(Romans 12:2)*

"And do not be conformed to this world, but be transformed by the renewing of your mind, that you may prove what that good and acceptable and perfect will of God is."

A community that has experienced pain and injustice needs forgiveness. Without sincere forgiveness, the anger and more accessible path of seeking revenge will consume the people and squander any hope for restructuring. Meaningful relationships in the community thrive where it is vulnerable-trust. We have to be deliberate about championing forgiveness (God's way) lest the undertones of years of affliction and duress are ignited by compounding frustrations.

Forgiveness is the only way to undo years of deliberate wickedness toward any given group of people and provide the possibility for communities to forget the past and work together for a better future without people waiting for a day to get even finally.

We have seen the lasting effects of unconditional forgiveness, i.e., which focuses on restructuring communities that have experienced significant pain (such as genocides). Communities, where widespread retaliation is not a far-fetched possibility due to the tangible anger and hatred between neighbors, have to vigorously and very intentionally teach the benefit of forgiveness. Otherwise, there is a chance of destroying all the hard work built by the generations before!

One of the testimonies of how forgiveness can impact a community is in post-genocidal Rwanda.

In April 1994, the violence during the Rwanda genocide saw neighbors murder neighbors. Family members killed infants and teenagers, mothers, fathers, and the elderly; all boldly murdered. World Vision estimated that about 800,000 people lost their lives in only 100 days.

Below is an excerpt from a paper *titled 'Confession' and 'Forgiveness' as a strategy for development in post-genocide Rwanda* by Anne Kubai retelling a survivor's experience upon encountering one of the perpetrators;

*"We sat in a small roadside 'milk bar' in Remera, Kigali, and we were deeply engrossed in a conversation as we enjoyed a glass of sour milk. A man then came and greeted her (with an embrace of the Rwandan style), and they exchanged pleasantries as usual. After he had left, she said that whenever she saw him, she felt something, even though she had forgiven him for what he had done. When I probed further, she said:*

*Did you not see that our eyes did not meet when we greeted each other? He confessed to killing four members of my family, and I forgave him because the church and the government told us to forgive. But I forgave him for what he confessed, and he knows that I know that he did not tell the whole truth. He also killed two of my nieces, and he did not ask for forgiveness for that. How can I forgive him completely if he does not tell the whole truth?"*

Stories like this are not uncommon in *'Umuvumu,'* a reconciliation program run by the Rwandan chapter of the Prison Fellowship as well as their 'reconciliation villages.'

*"Development in the post-genocide context entails more than mere civil co-existence. It requires peace that is accomplished through respectful dialogue and a willingness both to acknowledge the past and to look towards the future." (Hong 2014:7)*

There can be no healthy restructuring of the community unless the love of God penetrates our hearts as members of the community until we fully understand the responsibility we have towards society when we hold the power to forgive. We can never truly forgive without having the foundational understanding of God's unconditional boundless forgiveness toward us.

# Chapter Seven: 12 Benefits of Forgiving Others

***Blessed is he whose transgression is forgiven, whose sin is covered***

*- Psalm 32:1*

When God forgives us, we experience blessing. It is also true for those we pardon. So the benefits of forgiving others accrue to both the offender and the victim.

Here are 12 benefits of forgiving others;

1. Obedience to the LORD. There are many places in the scriptures where the LORD **commands** us to forgive those who offend us. Forgiving others is walking in obedience to our God.
2. When you forgive others, your heavenly Father will also forgive you. *Blessed are the merciful, for they shall receive mercy.*
3. You reflect God's character. When you forgive, you remember God's nature in you, which is love. You witness to the offender the abundant love of God!
4. It heals the pain in your heart. *A merry heart doeth good like medicine, but a broken spirit drieth the*

*bones.* Letting go of those who offend you removes stress from you, the victim, and the offender as well in cases where they are repentant.

5. You enjoy peace of mind. You let go of the bitterness; where your mind was preoccupied with the other person and how they wronged you, your mind wants the peace of God. When you're in un-forgiveness, you hand over the pen to your life; it's like taking poison and expecting someone else to die.
6. You do not give the devil a foothold. *Be angry, and do not sin: do not let the sun go down on your wrath, nor give place to the devil (Ephesians 4:27).* Anger indicates prior offense. Holding onto it will give place to the devil in your life.
7. You establish healthy relationships founded in love. And above all things have fervent love for one another, for "love will cover a multitude of sins" (1 Peter 4:8).
8. You promote vulnerable trust. You can be vulnerable to others about your weaknesses and failings; when you forgive others, you acknowledge that people

make mistakes, so you're able to be more vulnerable about your failings with others.

9. You gain perspective. You understand that people make mistakes and are therefore more gracious towards them. You also learn the value of getting the whole story, the two sides and making wiser judgments.
10. You inspire God's goodness in others. "Be ye good even as I am good"; when you forgive others, you teach others, those you influence—your family, your children, your friends— to showcase the goodness of God in them by forgiving as well when called to the occasion.
11. You encourage unity even among your other relationship. A grudge held between two people can cause factions amongst a community of believers or even a family and cause the people not to prosper due to disunity!
12. You can freely receive forgiveness from others (When you understand forgiveness, it is easier to receive forgiveness from others)

# Chapter Eight: Forgive Yourself

Now that we have come to the end of this book, I hope that your approach to forgiveness is more aligned with how urgently and importantly God esteems it. Nevertheless, I hope that after you have received God's gift of forgiveness, His amazing grace, you shall guard it and hold onto it so dearly. I pray that as you learn to forgive others unconditionally and truthfully, YOU WILL ALSO LEARN TO FORGIVE YOURSELF. Unconditionally!

***Love thy neighbor, as you love thyself.***

Since you cannot see what is inside people's hearts and minds, you'll often assume that everyone has it together and therefore be harder on yourself when you mess up. What makes it more difficult is you have all the incriminating evidence with all the detail put together and so stand no chance when you take up all three roles of judge, jury, and advocate! Forgiveness is an act of love; Love yourself so you can love thy neighbor!

I remember asking members in my missional community what that one forgiven sin was that confirmed that God unconditionally loved them. After a decade of silence, a few people volunteered to share a few of their dangerous sins, of course from years past, fearing that perhaps the leader would rethink their membership (kidding)! But over time, it is indeed easy to lose sight of the riches of God's mercy on the day you got born again and slowly fade into comparing the weight of your shortcomings to the abundance of His grace. The non-tither sees themselves holier than the drunkard, and the drunkard thinks they are better than the fornicator. The fornicator presents the prostitute as a more wicked brother, the prostitute points at the 12-time abortionist, who in turn points to the preacher and so forth! Weighing our sins against others doesn't make us any better than them. There is only one standard for holiness, and you and I are not it; God is the standard!

Do not partner with the devil. Forgive yourself. Be kind to yourself. Remind yourself that you are a work in progress and use those weaknesses instead to teach others about the saving grace of Jesus Christ.

*What have you been forgiven that proves God's love for you? What is it that threatens to revoke the remission of your debt? Confront it and forgive yourself! In Christ, you owe God nothing!*

It's easier to forgive others when you know that you, too, are fallible. Don't let your pride consume you. In the same way, you extend grace to those who mess up, you too can make and have ever made mistakes; minister that same grace to yourself. You, too, need the grace of God and are daily being transformed by the renewing of your mind.

When you learn to forgive yourself, you stop placing impossible or ridiculous expectations on those around you; stripped of the right to judge others by your submission.

*If our hearts do not condemn us,*
*we have confidence before God - 1 John 3:21*

# Works Cited

Kubai, A. (2016). 'Confession' and 'Forgiveness' as a strategy for development in post-genocide Rwanda.

Mukisa, M. (2017, May 11). Retrieved from https://mosesmukisablog.wordpress.com/2017/05/

www.ingramcontent.com/pod-product-compliance
Lightning Source LLC
LaVergne TN
LVHW050326160826
845677LV00014B/3543
* 9 7 8 9 9 1 3 6 1 0 0 6 3 *